Take Us Quietly

"It is always a pleasure to find Tammy Armstrong's name in the table of contents of a journal or anthology. Language in her hands can be trusted to lose its sag and wrinkle." — *Prairie Fire*

Unravel

"There are glimmers of the possibilities of language, a sense of the chase: Armstrong pushed the potential of the lyric into darker places, inside the seams of bar booths, where things get lost."
— *The Georgia Straight*

D1521395

The Scare in the Crow

Also by Tammy Armstrong

Poetry

Take Us Quietly
Unravel
Bogman's Music

Fiction

Pye-Dogs
Translations: Aistreann

THE
SCARE
IN THE
CROW

Tammy Armstrong

GOOSE LANE

Edited by Ross Leckie.
Cover images from www.sxc.hu.
Cover and page design by Jaye Haworth.
Art direction by Julie Scriver.
Printed in Canada on FSC certified paper containing recycled content.
10 9 8 7 6 5 4 3 2 1

Library and Archives Canada Cataloguing in Publication

Armstrong, Tammy, 1974-
The scare in the crow / Tammy Armstrong.

Poems.
ISBN 978-0-86492-627-2

I. Title.

PS8551.R7645S33 2010   C811'.6   C2010-902414-1

Goose Lane Editions acknowledges the financial support of the Canada Council for the Arts, the Government of Canada through the Book Publishing Industry Development Program (BPIDP), and the New Brunswick Department of Wellness, Culture, and Sport for its publishing activities.

Goose Lane Editions
Suite 330, 500 Beaverbrook Court
Fredericton, New Brunswick
CANADA E3B 5X4
www.gooselane.com

For J

Contents

I

12 Charlo — Ski Trail
14 Wanted: One Bearskin Rug
15 From Fundy Bank
17 Panther
18 Living Clock
19 Strange Apiary
21 Soursop
23 Porcupine

II

26 What Settles the Week
27 What to Do with Unwanted Keepsakes
29 Below Estey's Bridge
30 While We Sleep, It Snows
32 Diamond to Main
33 Highway Attraction
35 Nothing to See Here
37 Navigation

III

40 Failure of the European Starling
42 Dunbar Falls
44 Jökulsárlón: Ice Lagoon
46 Here: Soft-footed
47 Flight Stop — After Michael Snow's
    Eaton Centre Installation
48 Dim Sky
50 Speak Softly, Low One

IV

58 Dragline

60 Up-river a House Breaks
from Its Foundation

62 For you

63 A Pair of Horses: Those Ones

66 Patron Saint Against Lost Keys

69 River Scout

71 And She is No Stranger Now

73 Near Halfway — Swayed Both Directions

75 Where They Don't Belong

77 The Scare in the Crow

V

80 Hyla Amphibia

82 Grimsey Island

84 Lamprey

86 Zombie

88 Girls with Sharp Scalpels

90 Beauty to the Alligator's Beast

97 Canoe Lessons

99 Whatever You've Come to Get

100 On Renaming Mountains

102 This Late Light Tipping

104 Where it Softened

107 Acknowledgements

109 Notes

I

Charlo — Ski Trail

Out of the pine gloom
the fox pushed ahead of it all

into the sky's domed blare,
the field's fire opal.

White on white —
no colour wrapped the scrollwork of trees

along the Bay of Chaleur.
I waited,

stood chilled in my place.
Listened into the lost.

All beanbag and bunting,
the fox stitched and re-stitched the eyelet track,

the soft jag a hare had maybe left
in its swoon

before its cutty-shadow found the tree-well depths,
dived into the beneath.

The field was fire opal —
erasure in the open.

A crow tweaked its gunsight
and found only a girl in the middle of it all,

calling down the field.
The quartz in my voice

followed the syrup runs —
iced maples lacing the earth

in an off-beat claque.
Louder.

Waiting for that fox to return.
Waiting

while the wind had time to scrawl
so many glyphs in its passing.

Wanted: One Bearskin Rug

Splayed over the pine floor,
its split-dried paws once bunted autumn salmon
from the river, where maquillage and scale
weighted the light pewter.

The bear on the floor now snarls taxidermic,
stares off to the corner
where the dust and dog hair puddle
and the household tracks the pelt fine.

Wanted: one bearskin rug
with a mouth jawed in interruption,
thunderous —
before the blood drained off.

A territory then,
swamped in light and cross-breeze:
birches rustle their maraca canopy,
starlings chaffer in the sycamore loft

and bear, like a boiler tank corroded
at the subdivision's boundary, stands,
snout to the wind where something
sweats sour with one clear shot.

From Fundy Bank

Who thought you could slip the leash?
That small ending we found
in your death's coiling narrative was never clear
so we waited for you to double back,
collect your mail.

Instead, you ran the loon-note alone
to its final conclusion
until rippling mind-chatter
slipped you over night-smeared sphagnum
into the bay's dark escalator.

Only a year before
you were the pawnshop cyclist through footpaths
lamenting Vancouver's haltered dogs
yanking themselves toward
the cool drift from Masonic elms.

Peninsular.
For your mind, once steadied before the rift,
was an eroded vesper,
the forest traipse down to the blue bay skewed
in alder burr —
you needed a clearing,
birds squared away for the night,
the diving bell's untied bellow.

Only a year before we went to Culpepper's,
drank porter, smoked from one pack...

We all took the dogleg,
that predestined breakaway —
damned if you didn't step into that water without us,
already reaching for that something in the grey waves.

Panther

Over the years, hundreds of sightings of the graceful, tawny
animal, also called a cougar, mountain lion, catamount and
puma, have been reported from Nova Scotia and New Brunswick
as far south as Massachusetts....Wildlife officials say the reported
sightings actually involve panthers escaped from roadside zoos,
abandoned pet panthers or other animals, like bobcats or coyotes.

— *The New York Times*

Across the lake's shallow,
coyotes yip elegies
for prey stolen, territory lost,
for the panther's down-wind shush
across skidder trail dew-melt,
where trap sets trip open, empty out.

This sneakcat squatter
prowls the path five-star at the trail fringe,
watches with rosewooded eye
the children's zigzag trajectory
through the maize field cut,
watches the bungalows light on, light off.

Ferns billow the fugitive mantra
for the thunder drum that's still some miles off —
this deer tiger may slink through tomorrow's
chickweed field after the autumn burn —
ash prints sooting through crosswinds,
smudging our wildlife manuals' charts and tabs.

Living Clock

In his *horologium florae*
Linnaeus lunched by goatsbeard,
as scarlet pimpernel closed

and hawkbit yellowed the hour with forked bristle
while weeds and vulneraries worked a prediction
with time's vertebrae;

Linnaeus's star of Bethlehem motioned
from a pre-determined tilt,
his flowering tobacco furled

voluted leaves
for dark, admitted the evening
into ground slump.

The sow-thistle's thrive,
the botanical cog and wheel —
time through mineral seep and bloom.

Strange Apiary

To make a prairie it takes a clover and one bee,
One clover, and a bee,
And revery.
The revery alone will do,
If bees are few.

— Emily Dickinson

When the sun sheered the sugar maples,
we said *they were expected back.*

But midnight moves
left pocked carpet and loose-hinged cupboards.

Eidolons now to these outposts:
strange apiary

emptied of palaver and pollen ricks.
In the bee yard abbey

the Queen is missing still:
squired by libertines, perhaps,

she left the swarm and the domestics
tallying royal jelly rations.

Slipped off while the others lulled,
left neither note nor currency.

What of the almond blossom,
the groundwork blueberry bush

and apple orchard?
Last year was a choral cantata

inside the lilac bush;
the lilies roared heavy

with saddlebagged bees.
Now, nothing holds to basilica stem,

the architecture of plant.
Years ago the beekeeper beyond the orchard

caught us with mason jars
bedded with grass.

We never thought of disorientation
or the collapse of complex frequency.

We thought him a charlatan, a charmer of bees.
Now the caucus has left no census

and we crave black locust and fireweed honey,
a hum around our gin and tonics.

Here is where we go brief,
where the periphery expands

and we stand stupid,
our throats opening into a tone-layered *Oh*.

Soursop

The soursop,
ready,
split from the trees,

while the geckos finally claimed shade
between the plates of siding
and ceased their orgiastic chirping

over the terrazzo —
the day slunk heavy, refused to play.
Package tourists drank paw-paw cocktails,

thought little:
the photos and wooden trinkets
would be souvenir enough.

No mention of the guilt of boredom
that settled in the cabanas,
sifted the room with other winged indecisions.

The tourists' throats were braised with rum
and warm-bellied wants
as the doctor bird quickened past

in a gem-streaked torque —
its forked tail plying soursop
smashed beneath the tree.

The vacationers, tired,
absently followed Blue Mountain phrenology,
the taint of coolness that runnelled down their valley

from time to time.
The pooling though,
what to do with so much pooling.

Porcupine

Conspicuous fan-spray of spikes,
trudge of the self-conscious:
the anti-social rodent
happiest at sunset in the shadows —

exquisite limb-fall along the forest's funiculars —
brief aria in umbra.
It is lumbering determination,
knowing trees to bend,

others to step aside.
Regal in its robe of thorn,
searches salt from axe handles and bean cans.
Never crafted into child's toy,

disdained like a freak show caravan,
it switchbacks through yards,
past motion detectors
down Main Street.

We have all been the overdressed at the party,
the one rejected with tisking tongues:
girl with the large nose,
girl that could be pretty if only...

Lick out the salt.
See porcupine — gilded, sharp
in its thorny robe of seclusion.
Rock salt tipped and thickened,

its quills sway
through skunk cabbage pageantry.

What Settles the Week

Sunday. Empty. Open.
Men, downwind yesterday,
in their Mossy Oak camo,
owned this bird-shot sanctum —

      some hooked fingers into the sternums,
      opened up the birds like envelopes:
      wings and emptied flight dregs now,
      already seedy with alder bud, weed spore —

Yesterday, their dogs ran first light strong,
coursed the grazing fields to flush out wood bird —
hounds returning with the recall,
swamp-coated, mad for the hunt in it all.

But today, my dog, orange vested,
barges through the brush,
and we follow the leaf-matted trails,
the deep-treaded quad ruts.

These wings and spines in the till dust —
water-damaged
paperbacks with the covers torn clean —

these glimpses through bramble
(just glimpses, mind you)
apple orchards, sunken farms, words in pinfeather.

What to Do with Unwanted Keepsakes

None of us wanted it:
the groom's cake
wrapped in foil,
the gleamy brick of rum-soaked fruit

slipped always afterwards
into glove compartments
and good coats for the forgetting.

Does anyone still dream husbands
or is it straight to post-nuptial pleasantries?

If we're being honest
there's a lot of this going on,
the useless in the giving
while so much is breaking down.

Take this rib, here, for instance,
wearing thin,
the side you sleep on,

where his hand folds over
like a birthmark, an atrophied wing,

where you are afraid to speak in broken French
to his father who waits...
and you give what you wished you hadn't:
forked thoughts and the bottle of wine foul-up,

don't forget the foul-ups
that keep us renting on the wrong side of town.
Even at the dog park

it's difficult to breathe
when enthusiasts want to talk

about quirks and illnesses,
a predisposition, perhaps
— and the groom's cake
in your coat pocket,

becomes a thumb stone,
weakens the briar stitch seam
as the man explains his Airedale's dysplasia —

It's a mean piece of talk —
the on and on of it —

take those dogs running the fence,
pushing, shoving.
The whole world gaping.

Below Estey's Bridge

From the bridge's spandrel
and banks of pigweed,
headstones with sandblasted errata spilled

over into the river scuff:
their typos — resurrected Lazaruses —
meant a throwaway memorial, a rewrite

with the bereaved never knowing
how diamond saws cracked the granite
scraped out tangled vowels —

carvers with grade-school spelling
rushing out to their own lives at the end of the day.
I before e except after c...

Along the banks, I have scanned
these headstones for my own —
ice-split and spring-mossed —

my name, if only for a short time,
stamped on all stone and strong-armed
over the bank into the mineral rush,

and my surprise when the dates hinge and recede.
This chiselling in stone.
Just crow perch.

While We Sleep, It Snows

We are mortal, balanced on a day, now and then
it makes sense to say Save what you can.

—Anne Carson

You asked me again if I wanted to follow;
again, I pulled the duvet further around my body,
let the blind slap back against the window's frame.

Until that moment:
that last moment when you closed the door
and the house swarmed quiet,

I ran to say I would —
wait —
but you and the dog

already near the trailhead and lake —
the ice in your tracks sparked with light,
frost-glass from the Jack pines where dawn stained dark.

You moved toward the sun
and the ice moaned ecstatic
to feel its surface teased by you and the dog,

moving as though summoned
by another woman, another master
ginger-drawing you through open space into canopy.

Long after you'd both disappeared, the air puckered soft:
Here boy, best you come on home.

Diamond to Main

Charlie Chaplin shook a gentleman's agreement
for a performance, before the hill gospel sing-along,
but never made it to the coal mine village:
lost on the back roads,
went to Chaplin Road, Charlie Lake instead.

The village shouldered the spurn,
still went Sundays to the grandstand,
still side-listened
for the tap of a cane
on the paved side of Diamond Street.

That queer shape
sparking touristic legend:
Chaplin through the yarrow,
hemming the coal seams into a point of interest,
a village museum with keepsake brochures.

He could have been the currency:
a Stedman's Department Store
with Goody hair product displays,
and jingles on the county radio station.
And if he had performed:

the small theatre maybe tight
with bodies already rhapsodizing to their progeny
about fame brushed and those dark-haired children years later
penguin-tripping down Diamond Street —
fatherless, burlesque.

Highway Attraction

Remember that afternoon outside Culver City,
the great swindle of taxidermy:
the two-headed fox

and the tattered lamb with extra limbs.
Behind glass
the room was darkened

ambivalence —
shadow sharp,
it stuttered the sun.

We moved like the blind
from one freak to the next
through that grotesque menagerie.

What about those fights?
Debates you corrected:
act of wonder, act of wrath.

It takes three miracles,
like junk mail through the slot on Sunday,
a live burial:

always three days for a miracle to resurrect.
Culver City:
where the groom's cake dried stale

and we mired in another *debate,*
sidetracked ourselves
with the two-headed fox,

searched those imperfect creatures
for the stitches
that must hold such things together.

Nothing to See Here

Though the polio-twisted hand
has burled wood grace and the goitre

blistering from that woman's neck
is an astonishing tulip swell,

we are encouraged not to study,
not to stare into the infinite example:

the snapped brake line, the torn tread slur
that cross-hatches the scree

into whitescape, then down
into the development site

for the new retirement complex —
Mounties in rain-sodden authority re-direct,

keep traffic flowing.
We all have the evidence —

ghost stories that tally real:
anaphylactic shock

from sea bass, brain aneurysm
when he felt fine that morning,

or the girl in grade seven who fisted hair
from the boy's scalp. It fell: loose, free.

Abandoned owl prey, foolish on the ground —
a fallow cluster, auburn, fine

among the crabgrass violets.
See, we remember it like it was yesterday.

This is why we peel back bandages,
scrape tongues over chipped molars.

Feel here: please, believe in fragility.
Tomorrow may be different:

we may not wince when the hammer
overtakes the thumb,

when the other says, *it's over*
and the air lays us out

and the light slices us thin —
in the light, on the ground,

where the pain doesn't show
but becomes soundings instead —

our rawness standing close beside us —
she's the one who steps aside,

holds the door open, grinning
as though we've met before.

 Navigation

It was a half-note score,
a liquid symphony
that kept the songbirds at bay,
the yard masqueraded

as orchestra pit,
motorcycle tarp tympana.
A sustaining lilt
funnelled down the street grit,

pinged the *Caution Deaf Child* sign
like a spoon
dropped onto tile.
And when the gale finally caught

the screen door and whipped it
in tantrum against the house,
into the terracotta pots and gentians,
the dog managed a dry bark.

Like a spoon dropped onto tile.
There was a contingency,
an unexpected cymbal
in that wind-weary morning.

But the child did not hear,
the child without a hat
who dragged a lilac branch along the street,
dragged the silt-scratch behind her like song.

Failure of the European Starling

In spite of his remarkable success as a pioneer, the starling
probably has fewer friends than almost any other creature that
wears feathers.

— Rachel Carson

Say they're delinquent tax evaders
searching for cavities to nest:
old Fords, county-side mailboxes,
cyclone fencing like dark crinoline.

Say this rain's got to let up;
this sky sooted with steeple-twirp
has to end in something tailed bright.
Sure, Hotspur knew

a starling shall be taught to speak
but these ones —
released with all breed of bird
from Shakespeare —

babble like savants,
cap the yard in wolf-whistles
and corkscrew your Saturday barbeques,
three-martini sulk.

They are an 1890 legacy:
sixty from a burlap sack
loosened onto Central Park —
leader-dots, seeding morning,

stand now at two million,
speak in something
black-gated, less bardic.
These vagrant drill-soldiers

smear the sky with labour song,
find purchase in your hollows and salad bowls.
Like I said,
there's nature and then there's nature.

Dunbar Falls

We navigate by half sentences.

Our paddles snag duckweed,
bury our complaints in the plash,

in the forward push through
spatterdock surface-bloom.

At the stern, you steer round dark rock,
through the wind's muddled path.

Where did we stray from the cause
into Halicarnassus,

into the river pedigree,
where our dogs close behind,

insist on the whitewater turn —
surf hounds resting eventually

on the island pasture.
Sandbar willows creak

and cattle graze Hartts Island
bare through summer —

left for us to learn:
we are not water people —

the sumac candelabra tangles
the chokecherry in debate over debate.

We're still learning to duck the low-hanging fruit.

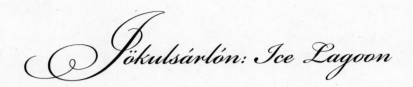

Jökulsárlón: Ice Lagoon

On the edge of it
calving ice
fractures into wrecking yard
while ice breaches elsewhere:

all of it an abstract menagerie —
sirenians
set off
in zodiacal light

as though the sky once sealed —
cloud and all —
so slow, so slow,
finally burst with too much shape.

Quick evictions crack the blue free.
Wolf bird: howling castrati —
that last kill-call —
locked in, released.

Echoes run rogue, stop short.
Walls cleave and crash.
And nesting skuas crimp the air with call —
they are antiphony,

rust song for spoondrift spray
and hunting geist.
Who knew ice held hymn
in cradled waters:

a flock of sky-starved creatures,
troubled in lagoon.

Here: Soft-footed

Out of Aldeberan's knotted light
the dog, the bear, the whale
spook haggard hope
while the pub here, at the Arctic Circle,
plays *Sweet Home Alabama,*

and the horses, weather-tied
to the water horizon,
champ the moss fields low.
This is the cinch in the light change
the waitress forewarns as she shoos us out

toward the driftwood church
and the latchings of bright salt
against the coming shade. It's the equinox
that creeps now toward these basalt cliffs,
grazing the light in its false turnings.

Sticks above our heads,
we stir the sky's golden fade
while a million birds fandango
their *joie de vivre,*
jackknife shadows with klezmer riffs.

We still live in our phobias, here.
And it's nearly autumn.
I have meant to send word
but the terns still run riot above clean thought
and my words are never my own these days.

Flight Stop — After Michael Snow's Eaton Centre Installation

They navigated poorly:
these black cherubim in the glasshouse,
fibreglass geese far from Thousand Lakes
into this given horizon.

Some might say a cathedral
without waterweed or lake landing
is a coming down into nothing
but escalators jig the din

and crowds shoulder through
for marked-down stereo equipment,
gold-plaited golf tees.
It's been years since this peregrination

found itself anchorage to the pleasure dome's
ceiling beams, a hovering in the light's unmooring
above those weekly dusted ficus
and amazon foliage pairings.

The big doors breathe in and out.
And all those movers and shakers
travelling in from milltowns, tobacco belts
walk the alcazar, finger instant tellers.

It's all just flight stop
above blow-out sales and a PA system
twittering Billy Joel Musak.
An eye-hooked velocity, just hanging.

Dim Sky

Under the LeBaron's hood:
a nest of bark strip and dryer lint
and birds where the fan belt should have been.
Outdoor-awkward,

we stumbled through our inability to locate breed
by wingbars or quirk calls;
our *Reader's Digest* guidebook quietly quibbled
with your choice: a chestnut-sided warbler:

The usual version approximates tsee, see see see swee BEAT chew.
With the last note dropping in pitch:
Several generations of birders have used "I wish to see Miss
Beecher."

Miss Beecher.
(Every rural route has its own.)
Her horses in the back field
run their jaws with bindweed.

Her blackbirds make a show of switchblades,
bicker out from old takeout boxes.
She's the sort to find the jagged in questions,
the sort who's always home (and this makes us anxious).

We needed time to regroup, reassess those slack mechanics.
It was the engine's almanac, the *Zsa Zsa* purr
that finally grounded the LeBaron on backyard rainwash until
the fall — old cars streaming bird, leaking spinster song.

Speak Softly, Low One

De mortuis nil nisi bonum.
Say nothing but good of the dead.

The dead are Townes Van Zandt on the stereo
in a swing-shift living room
with only the equalizer lights shifting frequency,

a guitar's thumb-picking about elsewhere:
something left standing in Tecumseh Valley or Tuscaloosa.
All that stateside mapping where things are apt to happen.

So it seems that we have come to the place
where the dead are not good shoes and pressed, black pants;
they are the leftovers from Sunday's roast,

the pot plants the uncle grows out at the dirt pit,
where late-night teenagers,
drunk for the first time on vodka and Tang, top the hill,

search for the chocolate factory's stack
and the loading bay's sodium light twitch
or further on: those cystic stars unloosening sky.

* * *

The dead are uncles found on dull Saturday afternoons
after cardiac arrests.
Nearly finished plowing out that second driveway...

Or hero uncles who died at eighteen in industrial accidents —
always handsome ones who drove fast Fords with sweater girls
and left old service revolvers wrapped in chamois below their seats.

We have learned to remain quiet,
hasp conversation together with the dogs that died years before:
When we had Laddie...

Around the time Prince and that coyote...
The vinyl purse clicks open,
a hard pack of unfiltered Marlboros tucked in the sateen.

* * *

A shawl of missing —
Grandmother no longer on the front stoop,
shadow of the clothesline like margins around her body.

She waves,
continues to wave until you have pulled out
onto the bramble-braided road.

She is still there.
In the rear-view,
she is still there.

* * *

Knotty pine havocked with eggshell oils —
layers chipped from white, to blue, to yellow to white.
The old cottage door hinged now to the barn.
The horses have been sold.
Stock trailers and the boys wrestling with the reins.
That was the year we bartered the buckskin...

* * *

Grandfather once bought a goat for the uncle decades dead:
Bought it for fifty cents.
A soft-tone hover in the kitchen

because the dead have been mentioned.
Subtle glance where Grandmother sat until last night:
fresh cup of tea before her.

No one sits there now.
Only the granddaughter drinks
tea with milk.

* * *

Because they come into the room by name,
linger into conversation
like Yardley of London and stubbed menthol.

One brief anecdote brings them
and they remain
while the living grow hesitant, willow-shy.

* * *

We go on after funerals:
aunts return to Florida
and cousins continue renovating in Ontario.

Do we come for the tally?
Because we remain:
successful, damaged,

shifted further down the line than before.
One less, one more.
The children are brought in,

but the older no longer fawn,
no longer try to remember names.
One more, one less.

* * *

So how many dogs you got now?
You look the same as you did at twelve.
Depending on how next year goes . . . we'll see.

* * *

There is a type of nobleness before the casket and pomp —
a grandfather in a nylon lawn chair
near the milled lumber for the garage

he's been waiting to build,
waiting until after *the good death*
when he can putter without worry.

How quickly his wife's body broke down,
softened into mulch-wood,
left her different in the bed.

In the yard,
in his suit,
he sits near the lumber, waiting

to go to the funeral
where the grandson who works on trucks will lead
the procession in an American car

and will forget the discrepancy between miles and kilometres.
Through downtown's speed-traps so quickly
he will lose the hearse and cars,

will pull over at a Tim Hortons
and wait in near panic for the others
to notch the hill,

past the highway of rimrock and pit run.
Follow him
through the lawn and cedar path to the plot.

The other plot because grandmother didn't want the junk
beside her: plastic flowers and wire stems,
Dollarama knick-knacks piled on Sally Mayfield's grave.

54

She will change the plot days before her death
because of clutter.
We'll say this makes sense.

* * *

That the minister miscounted grandchildren by two
and my mother took it personally
and my uncle was more concerned

with who sent flowers
than the casket being shut
is of no matter.

Though my family of workboots, work trucks
sat stiff in borrowed suits in assigned pews
and my mother chain-smoked after it all

though she'd *quit for good* last May
is of no matter.
Though I am unfamiliar to these uncles and cousins

many years now separated by country
and mountain ranges
is of no matter.

* * *

My grandfather takes a cup of coffee,
looks worn in his suit
beside the retired truckers and millwrights.

They small-talk about a palomino bought in Houlton.
A lifetime ago, he says,
stirs his reflection into the surface of coffee and steam.

IV

Dragline

The nine-million pound walking drag line, named after the female
character from the Robin Hood story and used by NB Coal in the
Minto area, has been moving slowly towards a new seam of coal.

— *The Daily Gleaner*

It was all for you and a childhood memory:
your father leading you forward
to the dragline's coal bucket
suspended in the fulcrum of progress:
this mega-machine skinned the land black
between coal palisades.

By June,
we'd dogged it south of Redbank,
shaped the story to say
this beast was spoor-tracked
to a buckled shale-band
but we hadn't planned any further...

so it waited
for our Moleskine notes,
triangulations,
swallowed the log-road
where the ravens snitched the slag pile tender.

Its rooster-footed pontoons
hashed the borrow pit,
snagged on brush-fire detail,
trenched lake bottom chassis and tailing—
still, we hadn't planned any further than this.

Maid Marian the locals call it:
head like a chain pickerel
locked in the hook-throes
jagged light cast back into our eyes.
Call it what it is: the broken road south—
snout to the seam-welt, diving.

When we find it,
it turns chantry
of the wildwood,
of the dale,
a cabin on chicken legs,
an old sow thinning terrain.

Waiting for it to turn,
we all complain about the cold this year—
stomp our feet,
wait for its footing to rasp the dirt:
its charging forward,
our stepping back.

Up-river a House Breaks from Its Foundation

It's what we've wanted:
cameras around our necks,
dogs around our wrists.
Toggled for the snow packs' unclenching,
we rubberneck the river,
search for what broke free:

a bungalow drama,
half-sunk in turbined slew,
shambolic patio furniture
thistled with shadow,
new kitchen curtains waving queeny goodbyes:
some envy in that kind of leave-taking.

Barricaded, we lean heavy
over our photography,
our swampy footprints,
watch the water eddy,
feel boondocked in the siren's zydeco
cherry-picking the side streets.

And the saddlebag preachers
washed in
from country churches make their rounds —
nomadic zealots in practical shoes
they muck and mumble a biblical limerick:
one hundred hymns on their tongues

and *we're in the eye of a robin storm now*
they sermonize from kayaks,
while hucksters fence sump pumps
and military personnel float water-dank
clusters of cattle downriver on cargo barges:
solemn to the passage.

This all took place before the river crested:
just bullhorn redemption
to our zoom lenses and expectations
for a washed-away house — a lumbered messiah:
TV antennae spoking above the roof pitch, staticky bright,
all of its windows blazing low sun.

 For you

There would be whooping swans
resuscitating the stilled afternoon
and fog like a punished hound skulking
the shoreline, the river maple's high-water mark.

And one glass eye from a thirty-year-old trophy buck:
one ambered skipping stone
with that thirsty, drink-it-down look
often found in my own eyes.

One glass eye: back pocket warm
where I biked home that night through the rain
to you who would speak no more to me.
It's late. Go to sleep.

For you there would be the raccoon's shadow
on its trestle bridge haunt,
tick-tacking girders and beams
damp in mooncalf slump.

And musky, bull-fencing the swing tide
ahead of the greening current
to make us just a little afraid
of brief migrations.

All of these rush the head's quiet:
our words bottlenecked
in that sort of mud-minnow shallow
strange gifts shape in backyard light.

A Pair of Horses:
Those Ones

Yet, mad with zeal, and blinded with our fate,
we haul along the horse in solemn state
>   — *The Aeneid*

Those months blued,
 dripped scarlet runners,
sheaves of marigold
against the fence gate

 while horses, buffed like saintwood,
stood the summer down
and we mad-dogged fieldwork—
clothes puckered with fescue and rough-twig.

Left with pastures flocked with crop-burn,
we goddamned all
the men out west in oil patches,
far from bad-tempered mornings.

Mean with still-dark
and dim rooms we read
for a particular sort of light
when light is always there:

candy dishes of light on card trays,
prints in the yard
mucked in high-strung coyote light.
There's temple in the stallion's

63

longbow vertebrae,
lappets of range,
a canter far from this
tin-banged farm shine.

But in our house:
knob and tube low wattage,
and hair walls —
the great equine engine

ceased and was scrapped;
in the spring the frost heaves cracked
the plaster and lath,
buckled the fieldstone foundation.

This house was
paper thin
the neighbour down the road complained
after we'd saved for *Beggar's Banquet*

and had played it over and over and over
on that turntable found in an alley out west:
paper thin
these walls that bucked and craned

toward the ridge line during high storm:
it was all just a wrangle
for space to roam —
back acres where the old Fords were kept for scrap

and grapeshot cratered the air in glass.
Hay dust still furred dawn,
crept the mantle-light:
all a corona hinged to wagon hub

that countersank scree and stag stone,
a space shovelled out for cart and Volvo:
it was the whip's *profundo* upside the sky —
double syllables urging

this roan assemblage into the silver birches
away from this house of swinging doors and canned food.

Patron Saint Against Lost Keys

Identify potential problems and possible solutions —
figure out what you're going to do before you do it.

To use the key,
to call this address *home*,
your mouth shifts, forms something different:
heliotropic.

When you came to the Province
and agreed to live in the never-finished house
with its bare bulbs and rooms littered with dishes,
this was not the life imagined.

On the counter: a Ziploc bag of keys
for deadbolts that stick in winter,
a bag of gold and silver —
meaningless out of context.

The one you need for the motorcycle
missing, the one that will send the Honda into idle,
take you down the river road,
past the petting zoo with the lazy-eyed alpaca.

Don't get on the bike after an argument.
Know your equipment.

Truth is, you hadn't expected this:
the unfinished, the unanswered.
Near-objects:
spice racks from old men in retirement homes.

Everyone misjudged, mispronounced where you'd end up.
Remember:
you're the type to leave men while on vacation,
walk out of the pool bar, keep going.

Is it a shoulder chip that keeps the keys lost,
the relationships unfinished?

Don't face directly into the sun without a tinted visor.

Oil paint of treeline to your left —
the road should be yours.
Past the repo auction house where men in plaid shirts
cluster around the awning, out of the light.

You'd meant to copy keys for lovers,
feigned forgetfulness when reminded —
entry has its consequence.

Truth is you mispronounced *heliotropic* —
lost focus
when the sun yawned the yard
out of shadow.

Counterbalance at speeds exceeding eighty kilometres per hour.

The keys where they belong:
on a nail at the back door,
on a nail in the plywood, cut from behind the oven,
to cover the hole left from piping,

an exterior faucet once planned for a garden —
a flower bed to hide the cascade of crumbling foundation,
the bike parts,
the lost keys.

The integrity of balance is found within the pit of the ear.
Lay into the road.

 River Scout

Even the dogs in West Kerry know that the 'otherworld' exists,
and that to be in and out of it constantly is the most natural
thing in the world.

—Nuala Ni Dhomhnaill

Even the dogs here fetch down the narrows between worlds.
Mine, asleep at the hearth, whimpers a river-sluice —
psychopomp to the limbo crowd
and their scrawled goodbyes.

He croups a threnody
out there for the ones who crossed the years,
who reach for his snouted insistence:
scratched ears, stroked scruff.

Mucking at the river's littoral,
they beckon and coo him passage
across that dark current,
shallow enough to touch bottom

until the middle —
riffled with hijacked spirit.
He twitches a hind leg
as though to shake off the damp,

69

then runs a meadow thought—
these daily visitations
when the woodstove's range burns red
and he dreams hot-pelted.

Through the river smalt,
silted where the path slides fast
into mushrooms and dark-seeded fruit,
he goes.

But what of the time?
Mere minutes here
but there enough to return overheated
near the birch-fed flames,

his heartbeat booted with kettle-tick messages —
arrhythmic meaning.
Nothing to me as I let him out to the yard
and he roves conscious

into the snow he's packed
into a sort of sense —
he vaults toward the fruit trees, releases
chickadees into tottery flight.

And She is No Stranger Now

For Amy Clampitt

But I say to her, how did you get here so soon?
How did you know the stonecrop is near frozen to the stem
and doe-eared shadows henna the hunter moon,
the limp phlox, and the rest hunchbacked in their bedded rows.

I waited to say, since you left, Amy,
Humbolt County holds women in trees;
they sleep in arboreal mythology,
in stands obi-knotted with logging tape.

Women with eyes to the low beam,
to the protesters' redwood canopy
and Maxxam Corp.'s helicopter hazing.
But a phone calls me to step from behind the door.

It is long distance
and speaks of harvest, harvest,
of a setting god,
a nurse tree rotten on the lee side.

You are no stranger now, Amy,
and you know why the sky keeps up its walkabout growl.
We tuck time into balance while you offer me
the same but different — the story that completes the story —

In Alpine Texas, 1955,
they flew a shaman in from California
to find water within the grove soil,
the moisture the city had lost faith in.

And in Falfarrias, it's the onions, watermelons,
cotton, and citrus fruit deep in that valley
where the frost roams in —
a cabbie skulking the dark glow numbering of houses.

And this wind shapes hackles onto the porch,
knocks the deadheads off their stems,
knocks the dog's dish into the dahlias:
silver bowl cleaned by crimson moon-fog.

And the women, Amy,
the women still in the joints of winded redwoods
keep the ring count knitted tight —
all this strangeness rooted deep.

Near Halfway —
Swayed Both Directions

All of it rain and ice swill,
the dam's excess.
Over the fields, tin-sheeted lawns,
sandbagged houses buoyed in reflections
inverted the welcome mats' infernal gab.
I thought to say that once

I'd scab-shimmied a culvert as a child
for a bet, the use of a bike or bat,
hunch-walked through the algae-slick
while the boys jogged the road above
to hang bat-faced
with their cartwheeled blood

pooling in the saucers of their skulls.
They waited and I paused
near halfway,
swayed both directions
to gather a bottleneck's worth of light
where the spring melt drained slushy.

In the middle,
the dark shouldered me
through the pipe's taunting echo.
I followed,
feigned conspiracy,
but the water, the dank

stays with me still,
deeper perhaps than skin,
the scraped palm.
Please. Don't leave me
to manœuvre this melt field
with its dark houses that nearly float.

We need dry land lit from above,
something at the end of the day
sure-footed.

Where They Don't Belong

Twitch light spindled swampland cottonwood
where the great toad grimace of a waxed moon
brindled the undergrowth,
made foreign the sapling den.

In the trees,
in owls draped in feverish study,
there were faces where faces didn't belong.
It's there, our minds insist,
so coax companions from quiet clearing
into snowfields rosined pearl,
where northerlies pitch-pipe the downs,
call dead friends out from shadow.

Too hard to tell what was watching what:
the great coniferous girth
of a bull moose jinxing the edge,
the coy-dog sparring backwood radials.
Faces here to keep us a little less static:
that friend some years gone
meddles near the hackmatack's trunk,
the snowbank's curvature.
Faces where faces don't belong,
where the airstream runnels a car's hood,
chirrups like wet wood crickets in the firebox—
bowing, stringing a sonata
empty of b chords or bass.

Sometimes a stump is only a stump.
Simply farm machinery,
wedding furniture tarped for a yard sale.

Simply a stretch of road and someone alone
with the *check engine* sign
cherry-humming
that jingle again.

But tonight is a hiking trail
toward a spring that free-pours
pewter at the next bend;
it means halfway.
It means light gulled between here and a treeline
pooling over watchdog verandahs —
ivoried, incandescent.

That dead friend cuts through shadow again,
leans against a mailbox,
wrestles the fire from a match head.
His face thrushes copper in your light beam.

That match head
finally freed from its cheap wooden frame —
crisping the everywhere.

The Scare in the Crow

Scrub-hobbled
in sky bloom and bindweed:

it's the scare in the crow
that's kept you here.

But Nootka lupine furl
will eventually pilgrim

this road in mauve rapture
and those wolf birds will flock

from *terra nullius* soon:
no more soulless than the rest of us.

Sun Queen, pine-boned in a Nordic sweater,
best to pull on out now —

they're coming,
those haggling vandals porched in oak.

Raised up on a church's pig iron toll
where the scare in the crow

leads to a river crossing,
fields brandied in testimonials —

they're coming.
Sure as hell to take you across.

Hyla Amphibia

Only cinder blocks and the jackhammer's
jittery grind before the unpredictability of frogs:
a kingdom animalia foreshadowing
our own sort of plague.

Down in the foundation's new-pour
mortar dust chattered the air,
fogged us distant,
while kohl-smudged frogs leapt the screed.

For a moment, a break in the reno-jive:
we were free to imagine our weight lighter,
our boot track forgivable
over curing cement.

We were the foregrounded rescue:
half-hearted messiahs
collecting frogs from the footing, brooming
a knot of leggy dark into a corner hamlet.

And from the egress, around the excavator,
we palmed each scroll-tongued creature
to the rhubarb patch —
its late season limp and decay,

its slump in garden preamble.
Those princely exiles, renegade Svengalis
shifted the fronds into imperial camp,
carried rain stone in their skin.

They left language in the basins of their throats,
faltered our machines, our small-town want.
In hindsight,
they were each the size of some animal's heart.

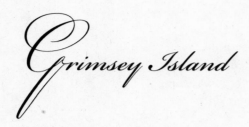

Grimsey Island

Stranger, that ticket in your hand belongs to me,
ocean-sick, wine-poor,

misreading an arctic catechism
under this pale nimbus —

the sun's over-stay.
Down there in the fog tangle the ferry waits for me.

And for you there is a truth here
among the glasshouses and winds accented north.

With your ticket
I'll be coastline by dark,

in the Southlands tomorrow,
to a church with prayer

owled in its rafters:
nothing to say but something to see.

You should think of staying here awhile
for caught inside all of us are birds

peeping from guesthouse guest books,
above this senseless shore of storm-chuck.

82

And all of our midge-specked meditations
need to work this out on islands

where no cats, no dogs belong—
the cats eat eggs and the dogs go chase-blind

across these rocks,
bawling the birds, the sheep over the edge.

And the air here smells like dogs
panting their gone-for-good mythologies.

Just before dark, the gulls and fish return with the men
but the fish air-drown in nylon nets,

and the gulls unlatch their mouths
like little red doors,

flash their feathered glide-ins
over serrated waves

gone grey in the dusk,
gone sky-ocean

where the combers empty out,
sharp as church-keyed tin.

Something to see,
if you'll just give me your ticket.

Lamprey

They say this is the lampreys' season
when females move slick-rock
into foundation —
a breeding ground

below the river boil.
St. John into Nashwaak:
we heave the canoe into
this after-work quest

for the lampreys' jittery path.
But to yaw, balk around:
two voices,
two directions.

The catbirds on the boondock signage
mew and thrush —
terza rima —
lamprey moves shore side.

You say,
It's dying anyway.
Whack the surface with your paddle.
Wait.

Wait.
Find it still alive,
still spring-wound propulsion.
We glide past the water purification plant,

try the J-stroke with lyric turn.
Divination in the river-theft,
and no witnesses on the root-locked shore
to your hunt,

your *hit that thing*-pursuit —
its sucker-mouth bobs ugly in the shallows.
I rest. You paddle.
Catbird double-tongues

what we mean to say —
it's the syrinx that keeps our voices
octavalent, distinct.
All this roll and growl

going on below us
is just mortar and brick,
cold-blooded masonry —
something playing the monster perfectly.

# Zombie

Say we'd die because *you're slow moving,*
not good in emergency situations.

Say this cinematic study of an abandoned farmhouse's
clapboard light
makes up the man and the woman,

makes the kitchen hutch and poster bed against a door.
Always the same motivation for raggy zombies

moving stilted and slow,
always a story written on EI stubs and hydro bill envelopes.

Here's to all who never got loose of ruts and patterns,
whose hands scratched wallpaper into Sheetrock,

where years of energy went to chopping, digging, dragging.
Went to jalopies, unemployment,

the money, the money, the money.
And here's to the bartered side of beef,

mealy raspberries, the garden stretched too far in pigweed,
the winter with candle and kerosene,

and the Holy Rollers at the door again,
again this afternoon —

blinking as they step through,
snapping birch bow past property line,

blinking out the clearing's light —
their vegetable ink pamphlets at their starched hearts.

The starlet screams —
hands over her ears to stopper the sight of zombies

breaking through, bringing light,
all those stories we work not to tell,

after those summer binges —
all those families forgetting the windows are open,

the sad stories running toward the river,
looking back, running for all they were worth.

Girls with Sharp Scalpels

Perched on silver stools,
we pried the organs free
until the glut of formaldehyde
fogged the room in tension headaches

and our probe
past scalpel and skin
severed the golden chapel's
mazy evolution,

folded backward a constellation phylum —
just swamp frog,
shipped from Tracadie
to lie spread-eagled on corkboard.

What kind of frog?
Just frog. Now strap on your safety goggles.
Find the two lungs.
Find the right atrium, no, right, your other right.

Check appropriate box on handout.
Answer me this:
What do you think is the function
of the nictitating membrane, and why?

This is what roughened the fairy tale,
left nothing graciously pinned —
grade ten droning forward
into electricity and blood circulation,

neglecting the plagues and bog prince's charm.
Still, our cache of silver blades hesitated the separation,
our uncoordinated language dismantled
McGraw-Hill diagrams and Disney dénouements.

Frogs from frogness.
They've spent centuries amidst the basement midden,
waiting for home renovations,
waiting for us to find them warted in regalia.

Beauty to the Alligator's Beast

The feather trade's cast of characters was a large one: in the big city, the fashion designers, millinery workers, salesmen, and retail merchants; in the swamps, marshes, and woods, the traders and plume buyers and, at the bottom of the chain, the plume hunters.

— Stuart McIver

I.

And just like my brother and me to work through Monroe County to get the reputation. Joined the Maximo Rookeries crew on a Tuesday — 120 acres near the mouth of Tampa Bay estuary; it was prime plume hunting.

The boys claimed 32 dollars an ounce for feathers. Same for gold. One ounce, LeChevalier said, equaled four egrets. "Tally as you bag," he said. "Tally it, boys, elle nous appartient."

Jean LeChevelier, *that big man, burned yellow brown, calm, with calm eyes*, that hunter became *persona non grata* — he was that one from Canada, and the *worst scourge that ever came to Point Pinellas.*

They say he travelled with a scribe only too eager for his slippery fable bending. He and Two-Gun Johnston ran the south. They ran us all:

old Confederates, outlaws and young ones who poled skiffs through those mangrove swamps and Seminole fog banks, dragging rations and breech-loader shot in hide sacks.

I'll admit we weren't sent to kill the pelicans at first, but did it in the off hours, fashioned their satchels into tobacco purses, before returning to cull the plume quarries.

Those nights in the overtime camps were blindfolds of oiled gunny and we needed all that drink to stupor their steeved croaks and cries. My hands still reek, five years after it all, of torn ibis and kerosene.

II.

Five years after it all, I still think of those birds on days when the harrows are fettered in rust-sulk or the snows keep the work dull. I think of them as broad guards watching us from a damp cypress branch.

Here, in the North now, the hardwoods are lean and I am beginning to forget the saw palmettos and slash pines, the Everglades' green water trace that met the horizon and held alligators and water moccasins beneath its calm.

Here, the land dries and October's sky yields saffroned time; my watch collects fifty-six seconds to your minute.

Still I make time to watch the geese fletch a chorus outside of the mean, toward rigour pointed south — my Florida.

III.

On my way here, I nearly touched some of those hats. In
Manhattan, a window display at a haberdashery. They were
millinery devastations built high: a variegated language,
a *nouveau animalia* in shadowy contortion.

Nothing like the shorebirds I sent forward. These ones held
wires and springs to make the birds move natural.

These hats were spring-loaded — a clockwork quarry inside the
shop. Mantles of gem-soaked arrangement, emerald and ruby
anthills.

In their wreckage, I catalogued grey swallow, peacock, and
pheasant bandeaux, ruches of coque plumes and spotted
pigeon heads — the birds stared out from cabachon and
baroque pearl — taxidermy tricking them alive.

And to say in ten years no one will wear them, *out of style, out
of fashion*: all those nuptial feathers hutched in the dim aeries
of border-town museums, the aigrettes — a spray of faded
flight —

They will be the fetishes of our extinct gods.

I tell you, Manhattan was only a well-heeled swampland.
Millions of dead birds and those women inquiring into cabinet
photo — *carte de visite* bathed in albumen and salt — their
heads posed just-so to keep those birds from tumbling into
the streets.

Eight years in. Five years out. Those spoonbills' and egrets'
flight feathers saw-bowed the sky.

IV.

My land, bought on the backs of birds. I roam but touch little:
frost on the stalk, the symmetry prayer in workaday dusk
pitches light onto the terrace like reading stones. That is what
I hear every night in the porch swing's ditty:

*At sunset with full crops they would move in their white thousands
and tens of thousands, with the sounds of great still silk banners,
birds in flock, birds in wedges, birds in wavering ribbons, blue and
white crowds, rivers of birds pouring against the sunset back to the
rookeries.*

V.

In our lantern-eddied haunts, the alligators kept close watch.

They found the hatchlings we failed to collect and their clabber
was chick-yolk glazing the roll-waves across the swamps.

In my Everglades, the bounty soured the awe. Those birds in
the kill space cried a coastal Latin soft. They were a woodwind
section seeped in vodka, a cacophony craning for asylum.

They spoke a quarry's novena, a breviary that never stayed in
print, rewritten each morning as the sun chose a lesser axis to
rise from.

Even from here, the North Country, they still call my name in
unaccented glossolalia.

VI.

*When the sun rose the ethereal whiteness of the plumed parent
birds shone like frost against the blue, blue sky.*

*They were white in the nights under the moon, or to the torches and
firepans of the men with clubs in canoes slipping along behind the
lights.*

Thousands of shearwaters spilled to earth, their bodies field
dressed where they fell: liver, heart, left to the sand, the ants
cleaned smooth the cloven shells. I have thought of this under
eiderdown with a fever that has tempered me into pooled wax
and my insistence:

I'm fine. I'm fine just where I am.

I have stolen from the Mangroves, I have snatched curlews and
egrets from the sky, torn them like butcher wrap.

And my boots those days never dried. LeChevalier walked
as though his Jac shirt were pegged to the sky, eyes raised to
calculate the profit in flocks.

Ounces of feather in colours he only knew the French for and
I only knew the heron was the hue of deep-collared water,
pools where light collected dust, where owls stuttered vole-
back hesitancy —

too much back story haunting our present tense.

VII.

In 1902, a London merchant claimed to hold 48,240 ounces
of plumes; this made for 192,000 birds. No one bothered to
count eggs or nestlings.

*By morning the bloody bodies would be drawing the buzzards and
alligators. The great black Florida crows that shed the light like
water from their feathers would clean out the dying young.*

*Ants in long lines as fine as pepper would carry off the rotting pieces
of their bones.*

VIII.

The Everglades became *paradise of plume hunters and the
purgatory of all birds.*

When I came out of the bayou without my brother, my
right eye already swelling from breaking that contract with
LeChevalier, I left the swamps sparked with uncatalogued
creatrix, amphibious gods.

IX.

Darling, I've borrowed more than you know. The Seminoles
have words for this but I lack a pronounce.

Though nightly I dream of my unborn children; they are small-
tailed gods with kites at their shoulder blades, learning to lift
off from the earth, learning to see the roam in the egress; *it's all
just beauty to the alligator's beast.*

I started these words to you from the anthem of a work
lantern, from a still-to-be-found crosscut where the guns go
mute. I wrote from the wreckage.

X.

I have heard from the locals of a breed of toad with fire opals
suspended from their skulls. And I have heard they are an
antidote, a correction for wrongs that cannot be forced into
rights.

If you see this toad will you write to me here? Will you be sure
to include notes on its worth?

Canoe Lessons

On the corrugated river
we put the dog in
and out and in

until it had no choice
but to lie in the bow
as we paddled toward the bridge

with its wind-plucked cables —
harmonics pitched to send the dog in circles
looking to fox out the sound, flank the tremolo.

Near swamped,
we worked past
the cottages, knock-kneed docks

and the apologetic stillness of islands
cleated to the sedge,
the oxblood fringe of blueberry fields and vetch.

Finally, the current weathered-out,
bucked us shoreside, near the bridge's after-shadow
and we dragged that borrowed canoe

through fern sway
and the green, green, green
inside our shoddy gallivant.

Upriver, the van still sat.
From hood to ground: crow-strut,
the others on the power line vetting for the last word

over the engine's heat stutter: *and, and, and...*
our bottles of water and sunglasses,
our keys left for the taking.

Whatever You've Come to Get

Has been given over
to the Sally Ann and thrift,
to the witch hazel reek of erasure
near the sink
where larder beetles, with their thin bands of gold,

loot the cupboard seams —
connubial, perhaps,
among the teaspoons and dessert forks,
the butter knives
tarnished along rose vine and fescue inlay.

Whatever you've come to collect
has already been reclaimed
for a restoration
by the beetles and vine dressers —
this kitchen has been given over.

Everything else
has been placed in apple crates near the alley:
memories of your childhood pets,
their collars and tags
shine brilliantly in the hands of scavengers.

On Renaming Mountains

Rush a mountain
and it will stand sulky
like a dog possessing a new name

(three weeks and the golden retrievers are still loose
among the foothills);
their echoes ring daily from the tablelands.

It's this sort of business that breeds fickle tantrum:
take Snowdonia's curvy princess massifs,
or South Hunan Province's Southern Sky Column

skewing the atlas now as Avatar Hallelujah Mountain;
even after Everest, Hillary growled,
Well, we knocked the bastard off.

But our mountains force us to send
goats and kestrels to the far banks;
in their pursuits across these barrens

they break in the new, unstitch the old,
circle for signature,
appellation in the banner-trees' lean.

In our mountains, the bull moose brays —
woods beamed with antler, the palmation of its breed —
it offers no allegory.

Its message is always north.
Name them north, among sobriquets and pseudonyms —
all these beatified trespasses.

Still, we coo softly to a christened range,
where the sun's slow pendulum unfocuses the face,
illuminates those shiplapped moods

we're apt to misinterpret,
those dumb-edged furrows
we've already mistaken for goodwill and open arms.

This Late Light Tipping

Hornswoggled by the season
the geese returned too soon
to Dunbar Falls where we legged the canoe
through ice pan

and the geese bitched palaver
across the fields,
stamped tantrums into shoreline snow
where an Elizabethan collar of slurry

wrapped the land mealy
and a frosty muskrat
played bo-peep with the hawk and osprey,
worked surface tension

with dexterous pageantry.
And with no real job to do,
we paddled the swill
with that dog who roved

through beer cans and crankshafts
on the bramble trail.
Until late afternoon tipped to cold,
ended our tooling around.

Last time along these riverbanks —
lost stables and harrows,
scrap trucks in wild rose cages come June.
These properties harangued in geese:

airships shadowing the earth's verglas.
These shore homes where nobody comes out —
all the rooms beaming lilac television glow
while slush lines unhinge in welcome.

This is our river now. Go on. Say it.

Where it Softened

You and the dogs had crossed clean,
but the ice wouldn't hold for a fourth.

So I shot down through ice hock with a sear—
not baptized but cleansed in the river maundy.

That sort of cold climbed into turquoise geometry,
staggered chest-deep slew—

while ice burn stellated my lungs,
left burred track in my bitching.

For a moment, I was something strange,
unnamed in seal's skin queer motion

and then you, already stripping my stiff clothes off,
wrapped me in your own warmed layers.

But listen,
by the time we reached the road

something gave,
wind spooled through the fir boughs foreign.

This, outside, stilled my complaining
and the back of my stammering tongue meant seeing

the ravens square their signature in the off-field,
wax the call, ignore our stumbling drama.

We got back to the road
without further witness.

And this place, come Sunday,
always so pressed with snowshoe-tramp.

Acknowledgements

Earlier versions of some of these poems have appeared in *Canadian Literature*, *CV2*, *Prism International*, and *Rampike*. "Speak Softly, Low One" was shortlisted for the CBC Literary Awards. Parts of this collection won the 2008 Tennessee Chapbook Prize and were published as *The Great Swindle of Taxidermy* in *Poems and Plays*. "River Scout" placed second in the *Eye Weekly* poetry contest. "Wanted:One Bearskin Rug" was nominated for a Pushcart Prize.

I am grateful to NBArts for the financial assistance that allowed me time to work on this collection.

Many thanks to Joey Babineau for his encouragement and suggestions on earlier drafts of these poems. And to Krista Harris for her daily trips to Sandholt Bakery and all those hatchback miles through Iceland's fjords ("Malbik Endar!"). Thanks also to Ross Leckie, my editor, for his suggestions, puns, and patience with reading so many, many drafts of this collection.

Notes

The epigraph for "Panther" is from *The New York Times* (August 7, 1990): "Naturalists Split by Panther Sightings in East."

The epigraph for "Strange Apiary" is from Emily Dickinson's poem "To make a prairie."

The epigraph for "While We Sleep, It Snows" is from Anne Carson's poem "Homo Ludens."

The epigraph in "Failure of the European Starling" is from Rachel Carson's article "How About Citizenship Papers for the Starling?" *Nature Magazine* 32 (1939):317-319. The italicized line is from Shakespeare's *Henry IV*, Part I. A hundred starlings were released in New York's Central Park in 1890 and 1891 by a group called the American Acclimatization Society as part of a project to introduce to America every bird mentioned in Shakespeare's plays. Today, in North America, the starlings' numbers have reached 200 million.

The italicized lines that describe the warbler's call are from *Reader's Digest North American Wildlife*. Pleasantville, NY: The Reader's Digest Association, 1982.

The epigraph for "Dragline" is from *The Daily Gleaner* (October 10, 2008): "Maid Marian's Journey Becomes a 'Drag.'"

The epigraph for "A Pair of Horses: Those Ones" is from Virgil's *The Aeneid*. Trans. Robert Fagles. New York: Penguin Books, 2006.

The epigraph for "River Scout" is from Nuala Ni Dhomhnaill's essay "Why I Choose to Write in Irish, the Corpse that Sits Up and Talks Back" in *Representing Ireland: Gender, Class, Nationality*. Ed. Susan Shaw Sailer. Gainesville, FL: University Press of Florida, 1997.

In "On Renaming Mountains" the Edmund Hillary quotation is from the article, "We Knocked the Bastard Off" in *The Guardian* (March 13, 2003).

The title "Beauty to the Alligator's Beast" is borrowed from Everglade historian Jack E. Davis as quoted on www.myfloridahistory.blogspot. com. The epigraph is from Stuart McIver's *Death in the Everglades: The Murder of Guy Bradley, America's First Martyr to Environmentalism*. Gainesville, FL: University Press of Florida, 2003. Other quotations are borrowed from Marjory Stoneman Douglas' *The Everglades: River of Grass*. Sarasota, FL: Rinehart,1947. Pineapple Press, 1997. Douglas was one of the first environ-mental activists who fought for the Everglades' protection; her lifelong work was instrumental in forming Florida's conservation policies. Details of Alfred LeChevalier's persona and plume camps came from Walter P. Fuller's article "Who was the Frenchman of Frenchman's Creek?" in *Tequesta: Association of Southern Florida*. Ed. Charlton W. Tebeau. xxix (1969): 45-61.